Easy Mint Cookbook

Cookbook

50 Delicious Mint Recipes

By
BookSumo Press

Published by
http://www.booksumo.com

LEGAL NOTES

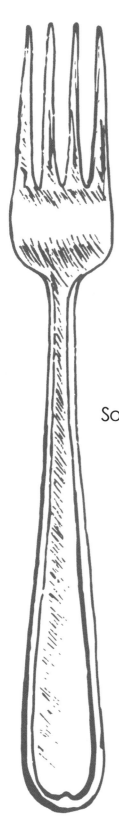

Table of Contents

Simple Lebanese Salad 7

Honey Garlic Salmon 8

Cool Fresh Jelly 9

Minty Honey Chicken and Spaghetti 10

Buttery Sweet Mints 11

Artisanal Handmade Cookies 12

Turkish Style Lamb with Mint and Radish 13

How to Make A Pound Cake 15

How to Make Brownies 16

Homemade Authentic Bavarian Candy 17

Southern Italian Style Eggplants with Bruschetta 18

A Mediterranean Lamb dinner 19

Mint Chocolate Truffles 20

Minty Asparagus Soup 21

Country Vegetable Casserole 22

Citrus and Mint Sunday Chicken Breast 23

Carolina 2-Orange Tea 24

20 Minute Potatoes and Peas 25

Catering Crackers 26

North Indian Inspired Chutney with Mint 27

Peppermint Candies Enhanced 28

Sweet Carrot Appetizer for 2 29

Manhattan Spritzer 30

Alternative North Indian Chutney II 31

Simple Candy Cake 32

1940s Style Milkshake 33

Grand Hotel Ice Cubes 34

Italian Mediterranean Mint Tomato Sauce 35

2-Ingredient Salad Dressing 36

Texas Cowboy Tea 37

Fresh Lemon Lime Cucumber Water 38

South American Inspired Avocado Salad 39

Country Summer Honeydew 40

Advanced Lebanese Salad 41

Tropical Mint Salsa 42

Wednesdays' After School Smoothie 43

3-Ingredient Central French Tea 44

4-Ingredient Georgia Juice 45

Frozen Summer Fruit Treat 46

4-Ingredient Lemon Dressing 47

Coconut Milk Rocket Smoothie 48

Telugu Lentil Chutney 49

Lunch Box Spring Tomato Salad 50

Easy Pierogies Turkish Style 51

Shrimp with a Creamy Lemon Sauce and Pasta 52

A Vegetarian's Dream 53

Winter Sweet Snap Peas 54

Mexican Soda Margarita's 55

Country Herb and Baked Parsnips 56

Northern California Summer Mint Curry 57

Fruity Guacamole 59

Simple
Lebanese Salad

🥣 Prep Time: 20 mins
🕐 Total Time: 25 mins

Servings per Recipe: 8

Calories	155 kcal
Fat	14.9 g
Carbohydrates	4.5g
Protein	2.7 g
Cholesterol	0 mg
Sodium	202 mg

Ingredients

1 C. walnut halves
1 lb. radishes, trimmed and sliced into thin rounds
3 tbsp extra-virgin olive oil
2 tsp fresh lemon juice

3/4 tsp kosher salt
1/2 tsp honey
20 fresh mint leaves

Directions

1. In a dry skillet, place the walnuts over medium heat and toast for about 2-4 minutes.
2. Then chop the walnuts roughly.
3. In a serving bowl, place the radishes.
4. In a small bowl, add the oil, lemon juice, salt and honey and beat till well combined.
5. Drizzle the dressing over the radish slices and toss to coat.
6. Stack the mint leaves and roll tightly, then slice crosswise into thin ribbons.
7. Fold the mint and walnuts into the salad and serve.

HONEY
Garlic Salmon

🥣 Prep Time: 15 mins
🕐 Total Time: 30 mins

Servings per Recipe: 4
Calories	481 kcal
Fat	31.1 g
Carbohydrates	17.5g
Protein	35.2 g
Cholesterol	114 mg
Sodium	2071 mg

Ingredients

1 bunch fresh mint, stems removed
1 bunch flat-leaf parsley, stems removed
1/2 C. fresh lemon juice
4 cloves garlic, peeled
2 tbsps honey
2 tbsps olive oil

4 tsps kosher salt
1 tsp freshly ground black pepper
4 (6 oz.) salmon fillets
2 tbsps butter, melted
1 lemon, thinly sliced
4 small mint sprigs for garnish

Directions

1. Begin to pulse the following in a blender: pepper, parsley, salt, mint, olive oil, honey, garlic, and lemon juice.
2. Work the mix until it is smooth then marinate your fish with the mix for about 10 mins.
3. Get an outdoor grill hot and coat the grate with oil. Then cook your fish on the grill for about 3 mins per side. Top your fish with some butter and serve with some lemon pieces and mint sprigs.
4. Enjoy.

Cool
Fresh Jelly

🥣 Prep Time: 1 hr
🕐 Total Time: 1 hr 20 mins

Servings per Recipe: 72
Calories	38 kcal
Fat	0 g
Carbohydrates	9.8g
Protein	0 g
Cholesterol	0 mg
Sodium	1 mg

Ingredients

1 C. packed fresh mint leaves, chopped
1 C. water
1/2 C. cider vinegar
3 1/2 C. white sugar
5 drops green food coloring

1 (3 oz.) pouch liquid pectin
9 half pint canning jars with lids and rings

Directions

1. Get a Dutch oven and add in: sugar, mint, vinegar, and water. Stir and heat the mix until it is boiling. Take the pot away from the stove then combine in the pectin and food coloring. Stir everything then put the pot back on the stove and get everything boiling again.
2. Once the mix is boiling let it boil for about 1/2 minute. Shut the heat then run the mix through a few pieces of wet cheesecloth.
3. Place your jars and the lids in some boiling water and let them sterilize for 7 mins. Now divide your strained mix between the jars leaving about half an inch of space at the top of each jar.
4. Clean the mouth of jar and remove any air pockets or bubbles then place the lids on the jars tightly and place the rings as well.
5. Get a heavy big pot and put a rack in it. Add enough water to the pot. Get everything boiling then once the water is boiling place the jars in the water carefully with some tongs.
6. Jars should be submerged.
7. Let the jars boil for 20 mins.
8. Enjoy.

MINTY
Creamy Honey Chicken and Spaghetti

 Prep Time: 20 mins

Total Time: 45 mins

Servings per Recipe: 4	
Calories	1054 kcal
Fat	58.8 g
Carbohydrates	92.1g
Protein	41.1 g
Cholesterol	203 mg
Sodium	417 mg

Ingredients

1 (16 oz.) package thin whole-wheat spaghetti
1 tbsp olive oil
2 tbsps olive oil
1 1/4 pounds skinless, boneless chicken thighs, cut into strips
1 pinch salt and freshly ground pepper to taste
1/2 C. dry white wine
1/2 C. chicken stock

1 1/2 C. heavy cream
2 tbsps chopped fresh mint
1 1/2 tbsps chopped fresh thyme
2 tsps honey
1 tsp lemon zest
1 tsp sherry vinegar
1/2 tsp salt

Directions

1. Get your pasta boiling in water and salt for 13 mins then remove the liquid. Add about 1 tbsps of olive oil to the pasta and evenly get all the noodles coated with the oil.
2. Get 2 more tbsps hot in a frying pan then begin to fry your chicken for 4 mins then flip the pieces and continue frying for 4 to 5 more mins. Coat the chicken with some pepper and salt liberally before cook it completely in the olive oil.
3. Remove the meat from the pan then add in your white wine and get it boiling while scraping the pan. Combine in the chicken stock and let everything boil until half of the stock has cooked out.
4. Now add: 1/2 tsp salt, cream, sherry vinegar, mint, lemon zest, honey, and thyme. Stir everything completely then again let the mix boil until half of it has cooked out.
5. Now add your pasta and toss the noodles then combine in the chicken. Let everything cook for 7 mins.
6. Add some more pepper and salt.
7. Enjoy.

Buttery
Sweet Mints

Prep Time: 30 mins
Total Time: 55 mins

Servings per Recipe: 24
Calories	165 kcal
Fat	7.7 g
Carbohydrates	25g
Protein	0.1 g
Cholesterol	20 mg
Sodium	54 mg

Ingredients

3 C. sugar
1 C. water
1 C. butter, softened
1/4 tsp peppermint oil

3 drops green food coloring, or as needed

Directions

1. Coat a jellyroll dish with butter then put the dish in the fridge.
2. Add the following to Dutch oven: butter, water, and sugar. Get everything boiling while stirring then set the heat to medium. Place a lid on the pot, and let the mix heat for 4 mins. Take off the lid get a candy thermometer and get the mix to a temperature of 250 degrees F.
3. Shut the heat and combine in your food coloring and peppermint oil. Be careful and avoid the steam. Carefully pour the mix into the jellyroll dish and leave everything to sit for 5 mins.
4. Get a spatula and begin to fold the mix over itself to cool quicker and let everything cool so that it can be handled.
5. Coat your hands with some butter then begin to work the candy into a ball then begin tugging on pulling the candy for about 7 mins.
6. Stretch everything into a long string then slice the string or rope into pieces. Let everything chill completely.
7. Enjoy.

ARTISANAL
Handmade Cookies

🥣 Prep Time: 20 mins
🕐 Total Time: 1 hr 20 mins

Servings per Recipe: 40
Calories	162 kcal
Fat	7.4 g
Carbohydrates	23.8g
Protein	1.7 g
Cholesterol	18 mg
Sodium	99 mg

Ingredients

3/4 C. butter
1 1/2 C. brown sugar
2 tbsps water
2 C. semisweet chocolate chips
2 eggs
2 1/2 C. all-purpose flour

1 1/4 tsps baking soda
1/2 tsp salt
3 (4.5 oz.) packages chocolate covered thin mints

Directions

1. Get your water, butter, and sugar hot in a large pot while stirring. Combine in the chocolate chips and let them melt completely then shut the heat and let everything stand for 12 mins.
2. Place the mix in a bowl, then one by one whisk in your eggs.
3. Get a 2nd bowl, combine: salt, flour, and baking soda. Combine both bowls evenly. Then place a covering of plastic on the bowl and put everything in the fridge for 60 mins.
4. Coat some baking sheets with oil then set your oven to 350 degrees before doing anything else.
5. Take out your cookie mix from the fridge and shape everything into small balls the size of a walnut. Evenly space the balls on the sheet and cook everything in the oven for 9 mins.
6. Place a mint wafer into the middle of each cookie, divide your mints into two pieces if the cookies are not large enough.
7. Enjoy.

Turkish Style
Lamb with Mint and Radish

🥣 Prep Time: 10 mins
🕐 Total Time: 3 hrs 43 mins

Servings per Recipe: 4

Calories	530 kcal
Fat	36.2 g
Carbohydrates	9.1g
Protein	39.4 g
Cholesterol	158 mg
Sodium	1759 mg

Ingredients

1 tbsp kosher salt
1 tsp black pepper
1 tsp paprika
1/4 tsp cayenne pepper
4 (10 oz.) lamb shoulder chops
1 tbsp olive oil
1/3 C. sherry vinegar
2 tbsps white sugar
4 oil-packed anchovy fillets

1 1/2 C. low-sodium chicken broth
2 tsps minced fresh rosemary
1/4 tsp ground cinnamon
2 bunches breakfast radishes, rinsed and trimmed
5 fresh mint leaves, finely sliced
1 tbsp cold butter

Directions

1. Set your oven to 275 degrees before doing anything else.
2. Get a bowl, combine: cayenne, salt, paprika, and pepper. Coat your piece of lamb with the mix evenly.
3. Now get your oil hot in a frying pan and begin to cook the lamb for 4 mins then flip the meat and cook it for another 4 mins. Once all the lamb has been cooked in this manner, place the meat to the side.
4. Set the heat to low and add in your anchovies, vinegar, and sugar. Heat and stir the mix and break the anchovies into pieces. Increase the burner temperature and keep stirring until you have a syrup then should take about 4mins. Combine in the chicken broth and set the burner to its highest level. Combine in the cinnamon and rosemary and get everything gently boiling.
5. Place your pieces of lamb back in the sauce top the lamb with the radishes. Place a lid on the pan then put everything in the oven.
6. Let the lamb cook for 90 mins then flip the pieces. Cook everything for another 90 mins, and then flip the meat again.

7. Increase the oven temperature to 425 degrees then take about the lid from the pan and keep cooking for about 17 more mins.

8. Place the pan on the top of stove carefully and place the meat and radishes on a plate. Get the sauce in the pan simmering and keep heating it until it gets thick while removing any excess fat. Add in your mint and butter and whisk the mix until the butter is completely combined.

9. Top your lamb with the sauce liberally.

10. Enjoy.

How to Make
A Pound Cake

🥣 Prep Time: 15 mins

🕐 Total Time: 1 hr 15 mins

Servings per Recipe: 12

Calories	498 kcal
Fat	30.7 g
Carbohydrates	56.8g
Protein	3.2 g
Cholesterol	156 mg
Sodium	135 mg

Ingredients

1 1/2 C. Idahoan(R) Original Mashed Potatoes (must be from the box, not in the pouch)
1/4 C. sugar
1/4 C. loosely packed fresh mint leaves
3/4 C. butter, softened
2 1/2 C. confectioners' sugar, divided
3 eggs

2 1/4 C. heavy whipping cream, divided
2 tbsps lemon juice
2 tsps grated lemon peel
1 (10 oz.) jar lemon curd*
1 quart fresh strawberries, sliced
2 C. blueberries

Directions

1. Add the following to a blender: mint and sugar. Continuously pulse the mix until it is combined well.
2. Now set your oven to 325 degrees before doing anything else.
3. Get a bowl, combine: 1 and 3/4 C. of confectioners and butter. Work the mix until it is fluffy then add in 4.5 tsp of mint mix.
4. One by one whisk in your eggs then combine in your potato flakes and a quarter of a C. of cream. Combine in the lemon peel and juice as well.
5. Coat a casserole dish with oil and flour lightly then enter the potato mix into the dish. Cook everything in the oven for 1 hour and 10 mins.
6. Get a 2nd bowl and add in the rest of the cream. Whisk the cream until it becomes thicker then combine in half a C. of confectioners and 1 tbsp of mint mix. Whisk the mix until it is peaking then add in lemon curd.
7. Get a 3rd bowl, stir: blueberries, confectioners (what is left), and strawberries.
8. Cut your cake into two pieces then top it with a large amount of the cream mix and some of berries mix.
9. Enjoy.

HOW TO MAKE
Brownies

 Prep Time: 10 mins

Total Time: 4 hrs 35 mins

Servings per Recipe: 20
Calories	208 kcal
Fat	13.1 g
Carbohydrates	22.6g
Protein	1.8 g
Cholesterol	16 mg
Sodium	88 mg

Ingredients

1 (18.25 oz.) package brownie mix (such as Betty Crocker(R))
2/3 C. vegetable oil
1/4 C. water
2 eggs

20 chocolate mint layer candies (such as Andes(R)), or more as needed, unwrapped

Directions

1. Coat a casserole dish with oil then set your oven to 350 degrees before doing anything else.
2. Get a bowl, combine: eggs, brownie mix, water, and oil. Work the mix with a mixer on low speed then layer everything into your casserole dish.
3. Cook everything in the oven for 23 to 26 mins. Take out the brownies from the oven and immediately top everything with the mints. Let the candies sit for 5 mins until they are melted then with a fork distribute the melted candy.
4. Let the brownies sit for 4 hours.
5. Enjoy.

Homemade
Authentic Bavarian Candy

🥣 Prep Time: 15 mins
🕐 Total Time: 40 mins

Servings per Recipe: 25

Calories	168 kcal
Fat	9.1 g
Carbohydrates	21g
Protein	2.7 g
Cholesterol	13 mg
Sodium	57 mg

Ingredients

3 C. milk chocolate chips
1 (1 oz.) square unsweetened chocolate, chopped
1 tbsp butter
1 (14 oz.) can sweetened condensed milk

1 tsp peppermint extract
1 tsp vanilla extract

Directions

1. Get a casserole dish and coat it with butter.
2. Add the following to large pot: butter, unsweetened chocolate, and milk chocolate chips. Let the mix heat until everything is melted evenly then shut the heat and combine in the vanilla, peppermint extract, and condensed milk.
3. Work the mix with a mixer for 2 mins then another 60 secs at high speed then place the mix in the fridge for 20 mins. Beat the mix 4 times during the 20 mins every 5 mins or so then take the out of the fridge and for 4 mins work it with the mixer.
4. At this point everything should be firm, slice the mix into small squares.
5. Enjoy.

SOUTHERN
Italian Style Eggplants with Bruschetta

 Prep Time: 20 mins

Total Time: 1 hr 15 mins

Servings per Recipe: 12

Calories	270 kcal
Fat	4.3 g
Carbohydrates	46.8g
Protein	11.7 g
Cholesterol	7 mg
Sodium	591 mg

Ingredients

1 (14.5 oz.) can diced tomatoes
1 small eggplant, peeled and diced
1 small onion, finely diced
2 tbsps dried mint
2 tsps dried basil

1/2 tsp garlic powder
2 loaves French bread, cut diagonally into 1-inch slices
4 oz. goat cheese, crumbled

Directions

1. Add the following to a large pot: garlic powder, tomatoes, basil, eggplant, mint, and onion. Get the mix boiling then once it is, set the heat to low, and let everything gently boil for 50 mins. Stir the mix every 10 mins. Shut the heat and let everything lose its heat.

2. Turn on your oven's broiler and place your pieces of bread on a baking dish and toast them in the oven for 4 min each side. Remove the bread the oven and once it has slightly cooled top each piece of bread evenly with the tomato mix then some goat cheese.

3. Place everything under the broiler for about 3 to 5 mins. Watch it carefully to avoid any burning.

4. Enjoy.

A Mediterranean
Lamb dinner

Prep Time: 20 mins
Total Time: 45 mins

Servings per Recipe: 6
Calories	490 kcal
Fat	33 g
Carbohydrates	29.5g
Protein	20.3 g
Cholesterol	52 mg
Sodium	357 mg

Ingredients

1 (8 oz.) package lasagna noodles
2 tsps vegetable oil
10 oz. ground lamb
1 tsp dried sage
1 tsp thyme
1/2 tsp salt
1/4 tsp pepper

1 (5.5 oz.) package crumbled goat cheese
1 bunch fresh mint
1/4 C. pine nuts
6 tbsps olive oil

Directions

1. Get your pasta boiling in water and salt for 12 mins then remove all the liquid. Once the noodles are cool slice each one into pieces width wise.
2. Get your veggie oil hot in a frying pan then begin to fry your lamb for 11 mins. Top the meat evenly with some pepper, sage, salt, and thyme, then shut the heat.
3. Add your goat cheese to the lamb. Evenly divide the lamb mix between your pieces of noodle then shape each noodle into a log.
4. Place all the rolls onto a serving dish.
5. Add the following to a food processor: olive oil, pine nuts, and mint. Process the mix until it is diced completely and evenly then top the lamb with the mix.
6. Enjoy.

MINT
Chocolate Truffles

 Prep Time: 15 mins

Total Time: 4 hrs 15 mins

Servings per Recipe: 24
Calories	120 kcal
Fat	6.3 g
Carbohydrates	16.7g
Protein	1.2 g
Cholesterol	5 mg
Sodium	25 mg

Ingredients

1 (12 oz.) bag chocolate chips
1 1/2 C. confectioners' sugar
1/2 C. egg substitute
1/4 C. butter, softened

1 tsp mint extract
1 tsp vanilla extract

Directions

1. Coat a casserole dish with some wax paper then get a double broiler going.
2. In the upper part of the broiler begin to melt your chocolate while stirring.
3. Get a bowl, combine: butter, confectioners, and egg substitute. With a mixer combine everything completely until it is smooth. Combine in the chocolate that has been melted then continue to beat everything. Add the mint extract and whisk everything again.
4. Add dollops of the mix by tsp into the casserole dish then place everything in the fridge for 5 hours.
5. Enjoy.

Minty
Asparagus Soup

Prep Time: 15 mins
Total Time: 35 mins

Servings per Recipe: 2
Calories	173 kcal
Fat	10.3 g
Carbohydrates	14.5g
Protein	9.4 g
Cholesterol	107 mg
Sodium	884 mg

Ingredients

1 pound fresh asparagus, trimmed
1 tbsp olive oil
1 shallot, chopped
1 tbsp chopped fresh mint
sea salt and freshly ground black pepper
to taste

2 C. chicken stock, or more if needed
1 tsp lemon zest
1 hard-boiled egg, chopped

Directions

1. Lay your pieces of asparagus on the counter and remove the tips from 6 of the pieces and place the tips to the side. Now dice the rest of the asparagus.
2. Get your olive oil hot in a saucepan and begin to stir fry your shallots for 5 mins then combine in the asparagus, pepper, salt, and mint. Let everything cook for 4 mins then add in your chicken stock.
3. Get everything boiling then set the heat to low and let everything gently simmer for 14 mins, then add in the lemon zest.
4. Grab an immersion blender and puree the entire soup.
5. Now get your asparagus tips boiling in water and salt for 3 mins.
6. Ladle your soup into bowls and top each serving with some tips.
7. Enjoy.

COUNTRY
Vegetable Casserole

Prep Time: 15 mins
Total Time: 1 hr

Servings per Recipe: 8
Calories   251 kcal
Fat   13.9 g
Carbohydrates   24.5g
Protein   6.6 g
Cholesterol   15 mg
Sodium   492 mg

Ingredients

4 zucchini, halved lengthwise
1/4 C. olive oil
3 sweet onions, chopped
1/2 tsp salt, or to taste
1/4 tsp ground black pepper, or to taste
1 C. short-grain white rice
1 (16 oz.) can diced tomatoes, drained and juice reserved

1 C. water, or more as needed
2 tbsps chopped fresh mint, or more to taste
1 C. chopped fresh parsley

Directions

1. Coat a baking dish with oil then set your oven to 350 degrees before doing anything else.
2. Remove the insides of your zucchini to form only a shell. Place the flesh of the zucchini on a cutting board and dice it then place it to the side.
3. Now take your zucchini shells and get them boiling in a pot of water and salt. Let them cook for 7 mins then remove the liquid then place the shells in the baking dish.
4. Get your olive oil hot in a frying pan then begin to stir fry the insides of the zucchini and the onions for 6 mins. Add in some pepper and salt then add the juice from the canned tomatoes and the rice as well.
5. Let everything cook for 6 mins until all the liquid is gone, while stirring then combine in the tomatoes and stir everything again.
6. Add your water half a C. at a time and stir everything until the water has been soaked up by the rice then add another half C. of water and keep doing this for about 13 to 16 mins.
7. Combine in the, parsley, and mint and cook everything for 7 mins. Place your rice equally into the pieces of zucchini.
8. Cook everything in the oven for 25 mins.
9. Enjoy.

Citrus and Mint Sunday Chicken Breast

🥣 Prep Time: 10 mins

🕐 Total Time: 20 mins

Servings per Recipe: 4

Calories	328 kcal
Fat	23.3 g
Carbohydrates	13.9 g
Protein	15.7 g
Cholesterol	34 mg
Sodium	302 mg

Ingredients

2 skinless, boneless chicken breast halves
- cut into bite-size pieces
1 clove garlic, crushed
1/2 C. all-purpose flour

1/2 C. margarine
1/4 C. fresh lemon juice
1/2 C. chopped fresh mint leaves

Directions

1. Get a bowl, combine: garlic, and chicken. Add in some flour to evenly cover the pieces then stir everything completely.
2. Get your margarine hot then pour in your chicken. Fry the pieces until they are browned then combine in your lemon juice and mint. Stir everything then place a lid on the pan. Let everything cook for 7 mins until the chicken is fully done.
3. Enjoy.

CAROLINA
2-Orange Tea

 Prep Time: 10 mins

Total Time: 10 mins

Servings per Recipe: 10
Calories   94 kcal
Fat   0.1 g
Carbohydrates   24.2g
Protein   0.4 g
Cholesterol   0 mg
Sodium   6 mg

Ingredients

3 C. boiling water
12 sprigs fresh mint
4 tea bags
1 C. white sugar
1 C. orange juice
1/4 C. lemon juice
5 C. cold water

3 orange slices for garnish (optional)
3 lemon slices for garnish (optional)

Directions

1. Get a serving container then add in your tea bags and mint pieces.
2. Add your boiling water over everything and let the tea sit for 10 mins.
3. Take out the bags of tea and also the mint. Add in your sugar and mix everything until the sugar is fully combined now add in your orange juice and stir again then the lemon juice and stir once more.
4. Enjoy the tea cold with some lemon pieces and orange pieces placed in each serving.

20 Minute
Potatoes and Peas

Prep Time: 10 mins
Total Time: 20 mins

Servings per Recipe: 8
Calories	89 kcal
Fat	3.1 g
Carbohydrates	13g
Protein	2.9 g
Cholesterol	8 mg
Sodium	163 mg

Ingredients

2 C. shelled fresh peas
3/4 pound new or red potatoes, unpeeled, cut into 1/2-inch cubes
2 tbsps unsalted butter
1/2 tsp salt

1/2 C. low-sodium vegetable or chicken broth
1 tbsp chopped fresh parsley
1 tbsp thinly sliced fresh mint

Directions

1. Get your potatoes boiling in water with salt. Let the potatoes cook for 3 mins or until they are soft then pour the hot boiling water over the peas and let them sit for 1 mins. Now discard the liquid.
2. Get your butter melted in a frying pan then combine in the salt, peas, broth, and potatoes. Stir everything and heat the mix while stirring to for a glaze. This should take about 8 mins of heating.
3. Combine in the mint and parsley.
4. Enjoy.

CATERING
Crackers

Prep Time: 10 mins
Total Time: 27 mins

Servings per Recipe: 40

Calories	100 kcal
Fat	5.8 g
Carbohydrates	10.6g
Protein	1.2 g
Cholesterol	< 1 mg
Sodium	< 65 mg

Ingredients

1 pound bittersweet chocolate
80 buttery round crackers
1/2 tsp peppermint extract

Directions

1. Get your chocolate melted with a double broiler for 17 mins while stirring.
2. Add in some drops of peppermint and stir it in then being to dip crackers into the chocolate mix then layer the coated crackers in a baking dish.
3. Once all the crackers have been coated evenly place everything in the fridge until chilled.
4. Enjoy.

North Indian Inspired Chutney with Mint

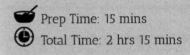

Prep Time: 15 mins
Total Time: 2 hrs 15 mins

Servings per Recipe: 28
Calories	11 kcal
Fat	< 0 g
Carbohydrates	2.7g
Protein	< 0.1 g
Cholesterol	0 mg
Sodium	42 mg

Ingredients

2 1/2 C. chopped fresh mint leaves
1/3 C. minced onion
1/3 C. white sugar
1/4 C. distilled white vinegar

1/2 tsp ground cayenne pepper
1/2 tsp salt

Directions

1. Get a bowl, combine: salt, mint, cayenne pepper, onion, vinegar, and sugar. Work the mix together until it even and smooth then place a covering of plastic on the bowl and put everything in the fridge for 5 hours.
2. Enjoy.

PEPPERMINT
Candies
Enhanced

🥣 Prep Time: 20 mins
🕐 Total Time: 30 mins

Servings per Recipe: 30

Calories	209 kcal
Fat	7.2 g
Carbohydrates	35.2g
Protein	1.3 g
Cholesterol	5 mg
Sodium	29 mg

Ingredients

1 (24 oz.) package white chocolate-flavored almond bark (melting chocolate)
24 peppermint candy canes, broken into pieces

1 drop red food coloring, or as desired

Directions

1. With a doubled broiler get your chocolate melted. This should take about 15 mins of heating stirring.
2. Get a blender and add in your candy cane and process the candies until they become an airy powder. Add the powder to the chocolate and continue to mix everything until it becomes bumpy. Combine in some food coloring and stir.
3. Place some wax paper in casserole dish then for add dollops of the mix (2 tsps) each onto the casserole dish then let the mix sit and reach room temperature before storing them.
4. Enjoy.

Sweet
Carrot Appetizer for 2

Prep Time: 5 mins
Total Time: 20 mins

Servings per Recipe: 2

Calories	173 kcal
Fat	2.2 g
Carbohydrates	39.9g
Protein	0.8 g
Cholesterol	5 mg
Sodium	107 mg

Ingredients

1/2 pound baby carrots
1 tsp butter
2 tbsps brown sugar

2 tbsps honey
1/8 tsp dried mint, crushed

Directions

1. Get a large and put in a streamer insert. Add in enough water to be right under the insert then place a lid on the pot and get the water boiling. Once the water is boiling add in your carrots carefully then place the lid back on the pot. Let the carrots cook for 5 mins then remove the liquid.

2. Get your butter hot in a frying pan then combine in your mint, carrots, honey, and brown sugar. Let everything cook for 4 mins while stirring.

3. Enjoy.

MANHATTAN
Spritzer

Prep Time: 5 mins

Total Time: 5 mins

Servings per Recipe: 4

Calories	174 kcal
Fat	0 g
Carbohydrates	46.3g
Protein	0.3 g
Cholesterol	0 mg
Sodium	16 mg

Ingredients

1/2 C. lightly packed fresh mint leaves

2 C. lime cordial

2 C. club soda

4 slices lime

Directions

1. Place a few pieces of mint to side for later then add the rest to a food processor. Grind the mints evenly in the processor then place your club soda in a pitcher with the mints. Stir the soda and mints then add in lime and stir again.

2. Divide the soda between serving glasses then garnish each with some of the reserved mint.

3. Enjoy.

Alternative
North Indian Chutney II

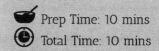 Prep Time: 10 mins

Total Time: 10 mins

Servings per Recipe: 8

Calories	13 kcal
Fat	< 0.1 g
Carbohydrates	2.9g
Protein	< 0.6 g
Cholesterol	0 mg
Sodium	150 mg

Ingredients

1 bunch fresh cilantro
1 1/2 C. fresh mint leaves
1 green chili pepper
1/2 tsp salt
1 medium onion, cut into chunks

1 tbsp tamarind juice or lemon juice
1/4 C. water, or as needed

Directions

1. Add the following to a blender: tamarind, cilantro, onion, mint, salt, and chili pepper. Work the mix into a paste then add in some water and continue to process everything to make a sauce.

2. Enjoy.

SIMPLE
Candy Cake

Prep Time: 1 hr 30 mins
Total Time: 1 hr 30 mins

Servings per Recipe: 48
Calories   71 kcal
Fat   3.7 g
Carbohydrates   9.7g
Protein   0 g
Cholesterol   0 mg
Sodium   45 mg

Ingredients

3 1/2 C. confectioners' sugar
1 C. margarine
3 tbsps corn syrup

2 drops peppermint oil

Directions

1. Get a bowl, combine: margarine, and confectioners. Work the mix until it is creamy then combine in the peppermint oil and corn syrup. Continue to beat the mix then add in some peppermint if you like. Place a covering of plastic on the bowl and put everything in the fridge for 1 hour.
2. Take out the mix and take off the covering. With your hand work the mix into balls then place everything back in the fridge again for serving later.
3. Enjoy.

1940s Style Milkshake

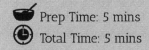 Prep Time: 5 mins
🕐 Total Time: 5 mins

Servings per Recipe: 2

Calories	231 kcal
Fat	5.6 g
Carbohydrates	36g
Protein	3.3 g
Cholesterol	21 mg
Sodium	74 mg

Ingredients

4 scoops vanilla ice cream
1/4 C. milk
1/4 C. chocolate syrup

1 drop peppermint extract

Directions

1. Add the following to a food processor: peppermint extract, ice cream, chocolate syrup, and milk. Process everything together until it is smooth then divide the mix between serving glasses.
2. Enjoy.

GRAND HOTEL
Ice Cubes

Prep Time: 5 mins
Total Time: 6 hrs 10 mins

Servings per Recipe: 12
Calories	< 1 kcal
Fat	< 0 g
Carbohydrates	0g
Protein	< 0 g
Cholesterol	0 mg
Sodium	1 mg

Ingredients

36 fresh mint leaves
2 C. boiling water, or as needed

Directions

1. Get an ice tray and place a 4 pieces of mint into each section of the tray.
2. Get your boiling water hot and then carefully pour the water into the tray evenly. Let the water sit for 15 mins then take out the leaves if you want, but you can also leave them for decorative purposes.
3. Now place your tray into the freezer and let everything freeze completely.
4. Enjoy.

Italian and Mediterranean Mint Tomato Sauce Topping for Cooked Meats

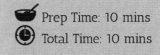 Prep Time: 10 mins

Total Time: 10 mins

Servings per Recipe: 6	
Calories	237 kcal
Fat	25 g
Carbohydrates	2.8g
Protein	< 0.5 g
Cholesterol	0 mg
Sodium	433 mg

Ingredients

2/3 C. extra-virgin olive oil
1/4 C. white wine vinegar
1 tsp salt
freshly ground black pepper to taste
2 tsps Dijon mustard

1/2 tsp white sugar, or to taste
1/3 C. chopped fresh mint
2 plum tomatoes, chopped

Directions

1. Get a bowl, whisk: sugar, olive oil, Dijon, vinegar, pepper and salt. Add in your mint then whisk everything together then add in the tomatoes and whisk again.

2. Enjoy.

2-INGREDIENT
Salad Dressing

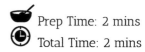 Prep Time: 2 mins
Total Time: 2 mins

Servings per Recipe: 4
Calories	4 kcal
Fat	< 0 g
Carbohydrates	1.1g
Protein	< 0 g
Cholesterol	0 mg
Sodium	1 mg

Ingredients

1 tbsp minced fresh mint leaves
1/4 C. red wine vinegar

Directions

1. Get a bowl, combine: cider vinegar, and mint leaves. Stir everything together then let the mix sit for 20 mins.
2. Enjoy.

Texas
Cowboy Tea

Prep Time: 25 mins
Total Time: 25 mins

Servings per Recipe: 12
Calories	102 kcal
Fat	0 g
Carbohydrates	26.1g
Protein	0.3 g
Cholesterol	0 mg
Sodium	9 mg

Ingredients

3 tbsps crushed fresh mint leaves
1 quart boiling water
1/2 C. instant iced tea powder
1 C. white sugar
2 quarts cold water

1 (6 oz.) can frozen lemonade concentrate, thawed

Directions

1. Get a serving container then add in your sugar, tea powder, mint leaves, and boiling water. Add everything in that order. Combine the mix to dissolve the sugars then let the tea sit on the counter for 20 mins. Combine in your lemonade mix then the cold water.
2. Divide the drink between serving glasses or place everything in the fridge to chill.
3. Enjoy.

FRESH
Lemon Lime Cucumber Water

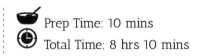

Prep Time: 10 mins
Total Time: 8 hrs 10 mins

Servings per Recipe: 8
Calories   10 kcal
Fat   < 0.1 g
Carbohydrates   3.7g
Protein   0.4 g
Cholesterol   0 mg
Sodium   8 mg

Ingredients

2 quarts water
1 lemon sliced, or as desired
2 limes, sliced, or as desired
1/2 C. mint leaves

1/2 C. sliced cucumber, or as desired (optional)

Directions

1. Get a bowl, combine: cucumber, lemon pieces, mint, and lime pieces. Stir everything then add in the water and stir everything again.
2. Place the water in the fridge to chill for 4 days. Make sure you stir the water at least once per day.
3. Enjoy.

South American Inspired Avocado Salad

🥣 Prep Time: 15 mins
🕐 Total Time: 15 mins

Servings per Recipe: 2
Calories	376 kcal
Fat	31.7 g
Carbohydrates	23.7g
Protein	4.4 g
Cholesterol	0 mg
Sodium	67 mg

Ingredients

4 C. fresh spinach leaves
1 C. sliced cantaloupe
1 C. sliced avocado
1/2 C. diced red bell pepper
2 tbsps chopped fresh mint leaves

1 tbsp mint apple jelly
1 1/2 tsps white wine vinegar
3 tbsps vegetable oil
1 clove garlic, minced

Directions

1. Get two plates, then place an equal amount of spinach on each one. Now place an equal amount of avocado and cantaloupe as well on the plates. Top each one with fresh mint and the red pepper.
2. Get a bowl, whisk: garlic, mint jelly, oil, and white wine vinegar. Work the mix into a dressing then top your salads with the mint dressing.
3. Enjoy.

COUNTRY
Summer
Honeydew

Prep Time: 15 mins
Total Time: 1 hr 15 mins

Servings per Recipe: 6
Calories   37 kcal
Fat   0.1 g
Carbohydrates   8.3g
Protein   0.7 g
Cholesterol   0 mg
Sodium   72 mg

Ingredients

1 C. cubed honeydew melon
1 C. cubed cantaloupe
1 C. cubed Crenshaw melon
1/4 C. dry sherry

2 tbsps chopped fresh mint leaves
1 sprig mint leaves, for garnish

Directions

1. Get a bowl, combine: 2 tbsps of mint, all the melon, sherry, and cantaloupe. Stir everything then place a covering of plastic on the bowl and put everything in the fridge for 65 mins.
2. Divide the mix between glasses for serving then add some mint to each.
3. Enjoy.

Advanced
Lebanese Salad
(Fattoush)

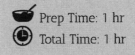 Prep Time: 1 hr

Total Time: 1 hr

Servings per Recipe: 6
Calories	257 kcal
Fat	17.3 g
Carbohydrates	23.5g
Protein	4.8 g
Cholesterol	0 mg
Sodium	138 mg

Ingredients

6 lettuce leaves, chopped
3 cabbage leaves, chopped
2 small radishes, minced
1 medium cucumber, diced
1 red bell pepper, minced
1 carrot, shredded
1/4 C. sweet corn kernels
1 large tomato, finely diced
1 small onion, sliced thin
2 large cloves garlic, crushed

12 sprigs parsley, minced
12 mint leaves, minced
1/4 C. olive oil
1/4 C. pomegranate seeds (optional)
1/4 C. pomegranate syrup
2 (6 inch) pita bread rounds (optional)
2 C. vegetable oil for frying (optional)

Directions

1. In a large bowl, add the lettuce, cabbage, radish, cucumber, red bell pepper, carrot, corn, tomato, onion, garlic, parsley, mint, olive oil, pomegranate seeds and pomegranate syrup and toss to coat well.
2. In a deep-fryer, heat the oil to 350 degrees F and fry the pita breads till golden in color.
3. Transfer the pita breads onto a paper towel lined plate to drain and then crush into small pieces.
4. Serve the salad with a sprinkling of the pita bread pieces.

TROPICAL
Mint Salsa

🥣 Prep Time: 20 mins
🕐 Total Time: 20 mins

Servings per Recipe: 8
Calories   43 kcal
Fat   0.2 g
Carbohydrates   11.1g
Protein   0.6 g
Cholesterol   0 mg
Sodium   4 mg

Ingredients

2 mangoes - peeled, seeded, and
chopped
3/4 C. chopped onion
3/4 C. chopped cilantro
1/2 C. chopped fresh mint

1 1/2 limes, juiced
1/2 tsp minced fresh ginger root
(optional)

Directions

1. Get a bowl, combine: ginger, mangoes, lime juice, mint, onion, and cilantro. Toss everything together completely.

2. Enjoy.

Wednesdays' After School Smoothie

🥣 Prep Time: 10 mins
🕐 Total Time: 10 mins

Servings per Recipe: 2
Calories	114 kcal
Fat	2.5 g
Carbohydrates	21.4g
Protein	3 g
Cholesterol	0 mg
Sodium	33 mg

Ingredients

6 ice cubes, or as needed
2 C. strawberries, hulled
1/2 C. kefir (optional)
1 tbsp fresh mint leaves

1 tbsp vanilla-flavored syrup
1 splash orange juice

Directions

1. Add the following to a food processor: orange juice, ice, vanilla, strawberries, mint leaves, and kefir. Puree the mix into a smoothie then divide everything between two serving glasses.
2. Enjoy.

3-INGREDIENT
Central French Tea

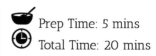

Prep Time: 5 mins
Total Time: 20 mins

Servings per Recipe: 4
Calories	4 kcal
Fat	< 0.1 g
Carbohydrates	0.7g
Protein	< 0.3 g
Cholesterol	0 mg
Sodium	9 mg

Ingredients

1/4 C. fresh lavender petals
1 C. fresh mint leaves

4 C. water

Directions

1. Get a pot and add in your mint and lavender pieces. Add in your water and get everything boiling. Once the leaves are boiling, set the heat to low, and let everything cook for 17 mins.
2. Now runt the tea through a strainer then drink the tea with ice and some sugar if you like.
3. Enjoy.

4-Ingredient
Georgia Juice

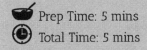 Prep Time: 5 mins
Total Time: 5 mins

Servings per Recipe: 1
Calories	232 kcal
Fat	0.5 g
Carbohydrates	60.8g
Protein	1.3 g
Cholesterol	0 mg
Sodium	19 mg

Ingredients

3 large peaches or nectarines, cubed
1 large apple, quartered
1 lime

2 sprigs fresh mint

Directions

1. Add all the Ingredients to a juicer and juice them completely.
2. Enjoy.

FROZEN
Summer Fruit Treat

Prep Time: 10 mins
Total Time: 10 mins

Servings per Recipe: 4
Calories	110 kcal
Fat	1 g
Carbohydrates	25.1g
Protein	2.2 g
Cholesterol	0 mg
Sodium	46 mg

Ingredients

2 C. cubed cantaloupe
1 1/2 C. ice cubes
1 C. red grapes
1 C. rice milk (such as Rice Dream(R))

6 large mint leaves
4 small cantaloupe wedges

Directions

1. Place the following in a food processor: mint leaves, cantaloupe, rice milk, grapes, ice cubes. Divide the mix between serving glasses and place a piece of cantaloupe into each one.
2. Enjoy.

4-Ingredient
Lemon Dressing

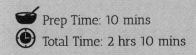 Prep Time: 10 mins

Total Time: 2 hrs 10 mins

Servings per Recipe: 4

Calories	161 kcal
Fat	18 g
Carbohydrates	0.7g
Protein	< 0.1 g
Cholesterol	0 mg
Sodium	1 mg

Ingredients

1/3 C. olive oil
2 tbsps lemon juice
1 1/2 tbsps chopped fresh mint leaves

1 tbsp chopped fresh mint leaves

Directions

1. Get a bowl, whisk: 1.5 tbsp of mint, olive oil, and lemon juice. Let the mix sit for 3 hours. Run everything through a strainer then add the 1 tbsp of mint that is left.
2. Enjoy.

COCONUT MILK
Rocket Smoothie

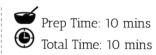

Prep Time: 10 mins
Total Time: 10 mins

Servings per Recipe: 2
Calories	173 kcal
Fat	12.3 g
Carbohydrates	16.2g
Protein	2.2 g
Cholesterol	0 mg
Sodium	21 mg

Ingredients

1/2 C. chilled coconut milk
1 C. fresh spinach leaves
10 leaves fresh mint, chopped
1/4 C. raw cacao seeds
1 tsp peppermint extract
1 (1 gram) packet stevia powder

1 banana, cut into pieces and frozen
ice, or as needed
water, or as needed

Directions

1. Add the following to a food processor: coconut milk, stevia, spinach, peppermint extract, cacao, and mint leaves.
2. Get the processor going then add in your pieces of banana gradually. Blending on into the mix before adding another. Add some ice to the smoothie and work the mix until it smooth.
3. Enjoy.

Telugu
Lentil Chutney

Prep Time: 10 mins
Total Time: 20 mins

Servings per Recipe: 16

Calories	16 kcal
Fat	< 1 g
Carbohydrates	1.4g
Protein	< 0.5 g
Cholesterol	0 mg
Sodium	25 mg

Ingredients

1 tsp cooking oil
1 1/2 C. fresh mint leaves
2 tsps cooking oil
6 dried red chili peppers
1 tbsp skinned split black lentils (urad dal)
1 tbsp coriander seed

1 tsp chana dal beans
1 tsp mustard seed
1 tsp tamarind paste
salt to taste

Directions

1. Get 1 tsp of oil hot in skillet then begin to fry your mint for 4 mins then place the pan to side. s

2. Get 2 tsps of oil hot in another skillet then combine in the mustard seed, chili pepper, chana dal, black lentils, and coriander seed.

3. Continue to fry everything until you find the seed sputtering then take the pot off the heat and let it sit for a few mins until you can safely handle the mixture.

4. With a mortar and pestle grind the mix into a spice then combine in the salt, tamarind, and mint leaves and mash everything together again.

5. Enjoy.

LUNCH BOX
Spring Tomato Salad

 Prep Time: 15 mins

Total Time: 1 hr 15 mins

Servings per Recipe: 6

Calories	110 kcal
Fat	7.1 g
Carbohydrates	11.9 g
Protein	1.7 g
Cholesterol	0 mg
Sodium	395 mg

Ingredients

2 large cucumbers - halved lengthwise, seeded and sliced
1/3 C. red wine vinegar
1 tbsp white sugar
1 tsp salt
3 large tomatoes, seeded and coarsely chopped

2/3 C. coarsely chopped red onion
1/2 C. chopped fresh mint leaves
3 tbsps olive oil
salt and pepper to taste

Directions

1. Get a bowl, combine: salt, cucumbers, sugar, and vinegar. Leave the mix to sit for 65 mins and stir everything once or twice during that time.
2. Now combine in the mint, tomatoes, oil, and onion and stir everything completely. Add some pepper and salt.
3. Enjoy.

Easy
Pierogies Turkish Style

Prep Time: 10 mins
Total Time: 20 mins

Servings per Recipe: 4
Calories   293 kcal
Fat   17.1 g
Carbohydrates   26.7g
Protein   9.4 g
Cholesterol   60 mg
Sodium   1098 mg

Ingredients

1 tsp salt
1 tsp dried mint
1 (9 oz.) package beef ravioli
1/4 C. butter
1 tsp sweet paprika

1 tbsp minced garlic
1 (8 oz.) container plain whole milk yogurt

Directions

1. Place your ravioli in a sauce pan with your mint, and salt. Let everything boil for 6 mins then remove the liquids from the pot.

2. At the same time begin to fry your paprika in butter with a low level of heat for a few mins then combine in the yogurt and garlic and stir and fry the mix some more.

3. Divide your ravioli between serving plates then top each one with the yogurt evenly then the seasoned butter.

4. Enjoy.

SHRIMP
with a Creamy Lemon Sauce and Pasta

 Prep Time: 30 mins
Total Time: 30 mins

Servings per Recipe: 6

Calories	396 kcal
Fat	9.2 g
Carbohydrates	57.5g
Protein	22.2 g
Cholesterol	111 mg
Sodium	422 mg

Ingredients

1 red bell pepper, julienned
3/4 pound large cooked shrimp, peeled
and deveined
1/2 C. chopped fresh mint leaves
1/4 C. fresh lemon juice
2 tsps grated lemon zest
3 tbsps olive oil

3/4 tsp salt
1/4 tsp ground black pepper
1 pound dry fettuccini pasta

Directions

1. Get a saucepan of water with salt boiling.
2. At the same get a bowl, combine: regular pepper, red pepper, salt, shrimp, olive oil, mint, lemon zest, and lemon juice. Combine everything evenly.
3. Now begin to boil your pasta for 9 mins then remove the liquid combine the pasta with the shrimp and stir everything nicely.
4. Enjoy.

A Vegetarian's
Dream

Prep Time: 20 mins
Total Time: 25 mins

Servings per Recipe: 32
Calories	24 kcal
Fat	2.2 g
Carbohydrates	1.2g
Protein	< 0.4 g
Cholesterol	0 mg
Sodium	39 mg

Ingredients

1/4 C. olive oil
3 large zucchini, thinly sliced
2 cloves garlic, minced
2 C. fresh mint leaves, finely chopped
1/3 C. distilled white vinegar

1/2 tsp salt
ground black pepper to taste
1 tbsp olive oil, for drizzling

Directions

1. Get your olive oil hot in a frying pan then begin to stir fry your garlic and pieces of zucchini. Stir fry everything for 5 mins then shut the heat and add in the pepper, vinegar, salt, and mint. Stir everything then combine in the olive oil.

2. Enter everything into a jar and place a lid on the jar tightly. Place the mix in the fridge for storage.

3. Enjoy.

WINTER
Sweet Snap Peas

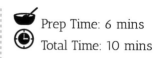

Prep Time: 6 mins
Total Time: 10 mins

Servings per Recipe: 4
Calories	67 kcal
Fat	2.4 g
Carbohydrates	8.3g
Protein	2.3 g
Cholesterol	0 mg
Sodium	75 mg

Ingredients

2 tsps olive oil
3/4 pound sugar snap peas, trimmed
3 green onions, chopped
1 clove garlic, chopped
1/8 tsp salt

1/8 tsp pepper
1 tbsp chopped fresh mint

Directions

1. Get your oil hot in a frying pan combine in the garlic, green onion, and snap peas. Combine in some pepper and salt and fry everything while stirring for 5 mins. Shut the heat then combine in the mint and stir everything again.

2. Enjoy.

Mexican
Soda Margarita's

Prep Time: 15 mins
Total Time: 15 mins

Servings per Recipe: 6
Calories	490 kcal
Fat	33 g
Carbohydrates	29.5g
Protein	20.3 g
Cholesterol	52 mg
Sodium	357 mg

Ingredients

1 lime, quartered
2 sprigs fresh mint leaves
1 tbsp white sugar
2 slices cucumber
6 cubes ice, or as needed

2 oz. white lemon lime soda
4 fluid oz. club soda

Directions

1. Lay out highball glass and squeeze and squeeze the juice of limes into it then add in the sugar and mint leaves. Stir everything together then add in the cucumber pieces and the ice cubes to fill the glass add in the lime soda and club soda and stir everything.

2. Enjoy.

COUNTRY
Herb and Baked Parsnips

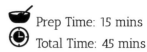

Prep Time: 15 mins
Total Time: 45 mins

Servings per Recipe: 4
Calories	154 kcal
Fat	3.8 g
Carbohydrates	30.3g
Protein	1.9 g
Cholesterol	0 mg
Sodium	375 mg

Ingredients

4 parsnips, peeled and cut into large
sticks
1 tbsp olive oil
2 cloves garlic, minced
1 tbsp honey

3/4 tsp kosher salt
ground black pepper, to taste
1 tbsp chopped fresh mint
1 tbsp chopped fresh sage

Directions

1. Set your oven to 450 degrees before doing anything else
2. Get a bowl and combine your olive oil and parsnips. Stir everything then top the mix with your black pepper, garlic, salt, and honey.
3. Stir everything again so the spices are evenly coated then lay everything onto a cookie sheet.
4. Cook everything in the oven for 40 mins then place it all back into the bowl. Carefully combine in your sage and mint.
5. Enjoy.

Northern
California Summer
Mint Curry

🥘 Prep Time: 1 hr
🕐 Total Time: 3 hrs 45 mins

Servings per Recipe: 8
Calories	552 kcal
Fat	38.4 g
Carbohydrates	28.9g
Protein	28.9 g
Cholesterol	59 mg
Sodium	612 mg

Ingredients

1/2 C. dried red chili peppers, stems and seeds removed
1/2 C. boiling water
2 C. grated fresh coconut
2 tbsps ground coriander
2 tbsps ground cumin
2 tbsps fennel seeds
1/4 C. peanut oil, divided
1/3 C. sliced almonds
5 stalks lemon grass, trimmed and thinly sliced
1 whole head garlic, cloves peeled and crushed
1/2 C. peeled and diced fresh ginger root
3 (1 1/2 inch) pieces fresh turmeric root, peeled and roughly diced

5 shallots, peeled and roughly diced
water, or as needed
3 tbsps whole star anise pods
2 (2 inch) sticks cinnamon
2 tbsps whole cloves
2 tbsps whole cardamom pods
1/2 C. diced fresh mint, stems reserved
1/2 C. water
2 lbs boneless, skinless chicken breast halves, cubed
2 tsps kosher salt
1 (14 oz.) can coconut milk
1 lime, juiced
1 pinch kosher salt to taste

Directions

1. Let your chilies sit in boiling water (1/2 C.) for 40 mins. Then remove the liquids.
2. Begin to toast your coconut for 6 mins while stirring then place the coconut in a bowl.
3. Toast your fennel seeds, cumin, and coriander for 2 mins then place the toasted spices to the side.
4. Get your food processor and puree the following: fennel seeds, 2 tbsp peanut oil, cumin, toasted coconut, and coriander.
5. Once the mix is smooth add: turmeric, chili, ginger, almonds, shallots, garlic, and lemon grass.
6. Continue to puree everything to form a paste. Then add a tbsp of water or 2 if you would

like to make the mix smoother.

7. Now add the rest of the peanut oil (2 tbsp) to a frying pan and being to get it hot. Add the mint stems, star anise, cardamom pods, cinnamon sticks and cloves to the oil.

8. Let the spice fry for 3 mins.

9. Now remove all the spices and throw them away.

10. Add the puree to the seasoned oil and cook the mix for 4 mins then add: 2 tsps kosher salt, 1/2 C. water, and the chicken.

11. Cook the chicken for about 12 mins until it is fully done then add in the coconut milk.

12. Get everything boiling and once the mix is boiling, set the heat to low, and let the mix gently cook for 75 mins.

13. Now add the lime juice, mint leaves, and some more salt.

14. Cook everything for 3 more mins.

15. Enjoy.

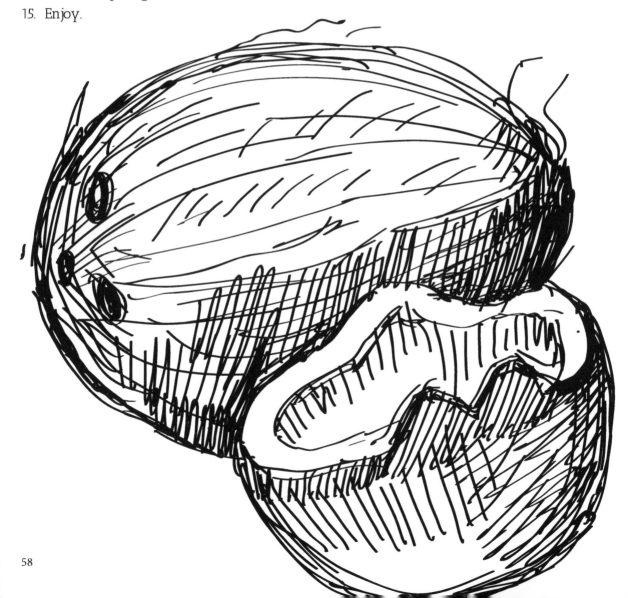

Fruity
Guacamole

Prep Time: 15 mins

Total Time: 1 hr 15 mins

Servings per Recipe: 8

Calories	98 kcal
Fat	7.5 g
Carbohydrates	8.7g
Protein	1.3 g
Cholesterol	0 mg
Sodium	55 mg

Ingredients

2 ripe Hass avocados - halved, pitted, and peeled
2 tomatillos, husked and chopped
1 ripe mango - peeled, seeded, and cut into cubes
1/2 small red onion, finely chopped
1 Serrano chili pepper, finely chopped
2 tbsp chopped fresh cilantro

1 tbsp chopped fresh mint
1 1/2 tbsp fresh lemon juice
kosher salt to taste

Directions

1. In a bowl, add the avocado and salt and with a fork, mash till slightly chunky.

2. Add the tomatillos, mango, onion, Serrano chili pepper, cilantro, mint, lemon juice and salt and gently mix.

3. Place a plastic wrap over the surface of the guacamole and refrigerate for at least 1 hour.

Printed in Poland
by Amazon Fulfillment
Poland Sp. z o.o., Wrocław